MW00441222

BEAUTIFUL SCARS

My journey
to
Wholeness and Healing

By

Brian Keith Anderson

Brian Keith Anderson

Copy editing: Spring Hawk Publications, (*a trade name of Rujiorva, LLC*)

ISBN: 13: 978-1477520734
       10: 1477520732

DEDICATIONS

This book is dedicated to my two sisters, Chantel and Kim. No matter how far down I fell, the two of you were always there to lift me up and continue to love me. Thank you for your unconditional love. You were the ones who taught me to love myself.

SPECIAL ACKNOWLEDGMENT

I want to thank my brothers Calvin L. Anderson and Daryl S. Anderson for being there through some of the darkest moments of my life. At times WE were all we had. We played together, fought together, laughed together and cried together. The blessing in all of that was – we were together. We went through hellish times but we're still here. It reminds me of the story of the three Hebrew children who were thrown into the fire, and how everybody who witnessed it just knew they were dead. But in the midst of the fire God delivered them. I may not say it as much as I should (my eyes are watering up even before I get it out) but I love you both with everything I got and I wish nothing but God's blessings on you and yours! One love FOREVER!

To my dad, Herbert Lee Anderson, for having the courage to go against all odds and take his sons away from an environment that might have led to their destruction.

❄

To my stepmother, Rose Anderson, for putting up with me and my mess, and for never ceasing to pray for me.

❄

To my late mother, Patricia Ann McCormick, who passed away April 11, 2010. She taught me the power of forgiveness, and not a day passes that I don't miss her dearly.

❄

To Jose Whitner, you have been a true friend for almost three decades. You never judged or gave up on me, and always lifted me up through the tough times. Thank you for encouraging me to write my story so that others might be encouraged and know that they too can recover and make it through just as I did.

SPECIAL ENDORSEMENT

By

Dr. Mary Ellen Copeland

"I am so glad that Brian is sharing his life story. It needs to be heard, and it needs to be read by all of us who care so deeply about people who are having difficult times. Brian is an amazing man, a giant of a man in every way and he has lessons to teach every one of us. His energy, enthusiasm and compassion is saving lives, and supporting people as they build new lives. We all have so much to learn from him."

Dr. Mary Ellen Copeland,
PhD, author, educator, and mental health advocate

SPECIAL ENDORSEMENT

By

Mr. Larry Fricks

From childhood despair and the hell of deep depression and addiction that almost ended his life, Brian Anderson has risen on the wings of faith, hope and recovery, fueled by his unconditional love and service to others. His is a story of inspiration of how high the human spirit can soar when we become servants of healing renewed daily by transforming the poison of our lives to medicine for others.

Larry Fricks,
Director, Appalachian Consulting Group, Inc.

SPECIAL ENDORSEMENT

By

Mr. Ike Powell

I was delighted to hear that Brian had a way of getting his story of recovery and resiliency out to a lot of people. It is a story that needs to be told. It is a story that can bring the light of hope and possibility to people who have lived their lives under the cloud of darkness and despair. In spite of the odds, Brian has not only come through, but has come through with a sense of power, direction and meaning in his life. He is willing to take on risks, challenges, and possible new struggles if it can move him in the direction he wants his life to go and if it offers new possibilities of service to others. As we say in the Peer Specialist training, 'When I see what you have overcome to get to where you are, I know that you are a walking miracle.' Brian is definitely a walking miracle who has decided that his life is about service to others.

Ike Powell,
Director of Training for the Appalachian Consulting Group

FOREWORD
By
Ruthie Jorgensen

"My life is not a curse but a gift, and a gift was meant for giving."

This has to be one of the most inspiring statements anyone has ever uttered. The above quote is one of the many beliefs and standards that Brian has chosen to live by. He has made it his life's mission to inspire and encourage anyone and everyone who happens to cross his path.

In the latter part of 1971, there was a well-known movie called Brian's Song. Though the movie was a story about another inspiring young man, and a different kind of tragedy, the title alone is aptly befitting the life of Brian Keith Anderson. His life has indeed become a song; a sweet melody that was once stifled by substance abuse and mental illness, but is now a symphonic tapestry beautifully woven by the hands of The Majestic Creator of the world.

Within the pages of this book, Brian chronicles his life's journey from the precipice of despair and hopelessness to fullness and joy that comes only from the realization that we are all created for a purpose, and that each person has a God-given, inalienable right to be emotionally complete regardless of who they are or where they came from.

From the deepest recesses of his heart, Brian shares in intimate, sometimes painful, detail the inward battle with his own personal demons and the travails that gave birth to the uplifting and inspiring man he has become.

As a Certified Peer Specialist/Certified Recovery Educator (CPS/CRE), he freely gives of himself so that others who are battling life's storms can experience healing and deliverance from the bondage of being enslaved by substance abuse, and other mental and emotional afflictions.

Brian also reveals how the road to wellness can be paved with many obstacles and temptations to, once again, become imprisoned and ensnared by the chains that can easily entangle those who are struggling to be free. He has devoted his life to the service of others and is a walking testimony that all things are possible to those who believe.

Everyone is willing to share their triumphs and victories, but few will freely share their failures and shame. Brian is unique in that he has opened his heart and put his life on display; inviting all to know and see his darkest days.

"A bird doesn't sing because it has an answer, it sings because it has a song."

-Maya Angelou

"There is no greater agony than bearing an untold story inside of you."

-Maya Angelou

GRATITUDE AND RECOGNITION FROM FAMILY AND FRIENDS

When I decided to go on the road, I knew I had to take my boys with me; there was no way I could have left them behind. We went through some very rough times and they each have their own story to tell. When children are hurting, broken and confused, sooner or later they will look for a way out of the pain, and that's what Brian did. But by the grace and mercy of God, Brian overcame, and is here to share his story. [sic]

Herbert Anderson,
Brian's father

❄

If you're reading this book you are the owner of one of the most remarkable, inspiring and life-changing books ever written. What I would like everyone to know about my brother, Brian, is that he has had an extraordinary life thus far. His determination and courage has made him unwilling and unable to put himself first above others. Family has always been first and foremost the most important thing in his life.

Cherry Parks,
Brian's older sister

❄

Growing up I can remember thinking that my brother was the coolest guy I knew. He wore cool clothes, girls loved him, and he was, and still is, very talented and can sing very well. However, I didn't know he had an addition problem until I began to get older and understand what was going on. But I never thought differently about him; he still loved and spoiled my sister and me. With all he's been through we never guessed he would be a part of helping people with their own rehabilitation process.

Chantel Anderson,
Brian's younger sister

❄

As a little girl I watched my brother struggle with substance abuse. However in the midst of all the chaos I knew my brother needed to be loved more than reprimanded. Due to continuous prayer for him, he was able to overcome drug abuse. Now I see him being called to speak to hundreds of people, telling them that there is a way to make it through.

Kim Anderson,
Brian's younger sister

❄

As his [Brian's] older brother I always tried to look out for him. Even now as adults, when we talk I'm surprised at the depth of the trauma that we experienced, and how it affected us all as individuals. In hindsight I think he was keeping an eye on me too… he became very protective of me. I could go on and on and on but I'll just say that we've always shared a special bond which continues to this day.

Calvin Anderson
Brian's older brother

❄

When God exchanges heavy for hefty, it is because He knows that the one entrusted with the reward will not buckle under the weight of prosperity as they did not buckle under the weight of adversity. This is the moment of actualization, when hope receives help as trial and tribulation give way to tangible abundant blessings. It is at this time when we may appear to be down, but because of Jesus Christ we're not out.

Daryl S. Anderson, Sr.
Brian's older brother

Brian Keith Anderson

❄

The support and advice I've received from this man [Brian] has been awesome. He's the prodigy of recovery; the mental, the physical and the spiritual aspects of recovery all in one.

R.C., Athens, GA

❄

I first met Brian Anderson in 2006. At first I didn't understand his recovery talk, but as I learned about Peer Support and what it meant, I soon started my own road to recovery. Me being diagnosed with schizophrenia at that time, I really didn't trust people. But thanks to Brian I started to recover. I started to take steps that I never thought I would take. Now I have hope, I love myself. Brian was a Godsend... he truly cares.

Recovery Outpatient, GA

❄

Arise, shine, for thy light is come, and the glory of The Lord is risen upon thee. *Isaiah 60:1*

For allowing God to use you is not only a blessing to us but you, yourself are being blessed. Continue to make a difference, but never change.

W.N.

❄

If I were writing a thank you note it would be simple, but how do you tell someone thank you for giving you your life back? Employee doesn't even begin to explain who Brian Anderson is. Brian Anderson is a man who truly cares about you. His commitment to us should be held up as an example for all others to emulate.

A sister soldier & Champaigne

To console those who mourn in Zion,
to give them beauty for ashes,
the oil of joy for mourning,
the garment of praise for the spirit of heaviness;
that they may be called trees of righteousness;
the planting of the LORD,
that HE may be glorified."
Isaiah 61:3 *(NKJV)*

Brian Keith Anderson

Recognition and Appreciation
by
Charles Willis

I have known Brian since 2004 when I became the Director of the Georgia Mental Health Consumer Network Self-Directed Recovery Project. My responsibilities were to engage mental health provider sites to allow a two-day presentation to peers attending peer programs. I contacted Brian who was the only Certified Peer Specialist at the VA Medical Center in Augusta, GA at that time. I had heard of the impact he was having in getting veterans to "think outside the box" to embrace recovery. Although, Brian was not a veteran, he was able to communicate his "lived experience" and model recovery in such a way that the veterans became open-minded enough to listen to his message. As a result of building trust among this group of veterans he sought resources from the Georgia Mental Health Consumer Network, public and private agencies to introduce recovery concepts to these individuals. This was a tremendous hurdle to overcome.

Brian consistently provided training to this population to enhance their interpersonal relationships with clinicians, therapist, and most of all family members who were directly impacted by emotions and behaviors of these individuals. When I presented the Wellness Recovery Action Plan (WRAP) to the group I was met with resistance although I was a person living with a mental health diagnosis. It was because of Brian's sincere empathetic approach of understanding this veteran population and communicating his intention of providing them with choices in their lives that made the difference in the veteran peers' ability to listen to the presentation and embrace its concepts. I was subsequently invited back to a Peer Education Program at the VA Hospital in Augusta, where Brian and members of the peer group put together a facility/community program to share what had been gained from participating in the peer program that Certified Peer Specialist, Brian Anderson had developed. The veteran participants shared their concepts of what recovery meant to them, and shared about the intimate relationships they had kindled with each other. Family members in the audience expressed the relief they were experiencing at home living with their recovery oriented husbands. They echoed the same sentiments as many of their husbands when they talked about the behavioral changes they were experiencing at home since the creation and formation of the peer program designed and implemented by Brian's efforts. Staff shared their experiences of working with the veterans in a more mutually respectful manner. They too discussed how the mental health services had improved since the initiation of the peer project.

At last year's conference Brian along with members of the veterans peer group provided the audience with a musical performance that "brought the roof down". Brian has continued to develop as a Certified Peer Specialist focusing his efforts on providing Cultural Competence Training and education to peers participating in the Certified Peer Specialist Training. He has demonstrated the capacity to provide effortless support to the VA Peer Program participants and his peers across the State and the Nation. I am very proud to share the credential of a Certified Peer Specialist with people like Brian and I too want to be able to exceed among my peer group. As I travel throughout the United States and interface with veterans I find that Brian Anderson is synonymous with the VA Peer Support Programs.

If I can overcome, anyone can.
If I can make it to the light at the end of
the tunnel, so can you.

May this book be a blessing to you as
you read through the pages of my life.

Your friend in recovery,
Brian Keith Anderson

CHAPTER ONE

My earliest childhood memories began at the tender age of five. It was the early 1970's and I remember having a close-knit family where both mom and dad nurtured us children and kept the home fires burning. My parents were practically children themselves when they married, and I was their youngest at that time. We lived in the projects of Jersey City, New Jersey. Most people are quick to attach a stigma or stereotypical dysfunction to living in the projects. But the prevalence of love and unity in our household eclipsed any shadow of what, by most standards, would be deemed an undesirable or underprivileged living environment. In fact, my family was considered upper echelon; pillars of the community, and the envy of many other families in the neighborhood. When I reminisce about the happy times, I remember the simple pleasures that made home, home. Seems it's always the simple things that remain forever etched in the mind of a troubled child, and those are the things that are most often taken for

3

granted by everyone else. Life's trials and hardships have not erased or contaminated my memories of the good times. It's what you might call "keepsake memories"... like being awakened by the mesmerizing aroma of bacon frying in the morning, or the fragrant bouquet of laundry dried in the sweet smell of a fresh springtime breeze. These are the memories you try your best to hold on to; you lock them away in the vault hidden deep within your soul and preserve them throughout your life as a source of comfort and strength when everything else in your world becomes dark and dismal.

It was still early in the 1970s when my father made a life-changing decision to begin a spiritual walk. He committed his life to God and to the Church. He was dedicated and devoted to living a Godly life at any cost. At times, his unwavering commitment to the Church superseded everything else. It even prevented him from working certain jobs because he adamantly refused to encroach on his holy day with any other activity that wasn't Church-related. By all accounts, a spiritual commitment such as this should have been the best thing that could have happened in anyone's life, or in any family. And, yes, on the surface, to the casual observer, it was. It seemed as if the Anderson family had it all together. We were already perceived as a unified, model family, and added to that, we had become religiously reinforced. Or so it seemed. But inside the hallowed walls of our home, life was very different from how it appeared from the outside.

The realities of life are never crystal clear in the mind of a child, but I can still remember that prior to my father's total conversion, my parents enjoyed the social scene; they partied and had a good time together. Then suddenly dad was leaving all that behind and turning over a new leaf. He was beginning a new chapter where the Church was the epicenter of his life. My father's transformation began when his mother invited him to a tent meeting held by her pastor, who wasn't much older than my father was at that time. Dad said when he heard the pastor's message he was hooked, and went back every night for the next six weeks. His devotion to the Church was initially met with resistance by my mother who wasn't quite as eager as he was to embrace this new life. Even though she eventually accepted his decision and attended Church with him, it was clear that there was a rift between them. Their differences gradually began to take a toll on their marriage and the overall harmony of the household.

It had become a yearly tradition for our family to go to Pottstown, PA for the annual camp meeting (a religious gathering that people would travel from all parts of the country to attend). It was a time of spiritual revival and refreshing, and was a fundamental building block in the life of the believer. Like clockwork every summer, we packed our suitcases, loaded into the car and headed off to camp meeting. But as my parents' marriage deteriorated, the yearly road trip suddenly changed. One particular year, under the guise of keeping the annual Pottstown tradition, my father led my mother to believe that he was still planning on making the trip with just us boys. But in reality his true destination was Seattle, WA. His plan was to take his sons as far away from New Jersey as he could possibly get them. So, that year my two older brothers and I left with my dad—believing that we were headed to camp meeting. My mother and older sister stayed behind.

Near as I can recall, it was around this same time that my parents formally separated, and it was by no means a harmonious split. It was a separation wrought with mudslinging, spite and the worst kind of hurtful drama. So the _supposed_ trip to camp meeting that year was a welcomed escape for everyone. It gave us all a much-needed getaway from the conflict and turmoil that was surging through our family.

So, dad loaded my brothers and me in the car, and we headed out of New Jersey in route to Seattle, WA. But we never made it to Seattle, we ran out of gas and money in Ohio. In retrospect, dad's destination may or may not have been Seattle. He may not have had a destination in mind at all. His goal might have just been to take his sons away from there and end up wherever we ended up. Looking back at that point in time it's hard to say. But one thing was for certain, and that was my father's resolve to protect and save his sons at any cost. He was devoted to us boys and wanted us with him no matter what.

So, there we were. I was five years old, my brothers were seven and nine, and we were stranded in Ohio with our father. The four of us spent many uncomfortable nights sleeping in the car. To earn money for food, dad would sell Christian books and literature to various Churches, retail outlets, and sometimes just door-to-door. In the process of selling these books, he would sometimes meet people who were willing to lend a helping hand to him and his boys. Some would even generously allow us to spend a night or two in their homes, which was a welcomed alternative to roughing it night after night in the car. We scored big when we met this wonderful, kindhearted woman who had five children of her own but not much else. Her hovel-like house was barely standing but she welcomed us in. Even though it was shabby and in a state of serious disrepair, it gave me a shred of stability and family life I so desperately needed at that time. The sum total of both our families' material possessions "combined" still equaled practically nothing. But this dear lady treated us like she treated her own children, and for about two years, I felt a sense of belonging, warmth and security. But that feeling came to an abrupt end when my father decided to pursue a theology degree and go into full time ministry. That meant uprooting us from Ohio—leaving the place that had been a source of stability for the last two years and heading for Huntsville, AL, where dad would attend a private Christian college. I was still a very young child (about eight years old), and the exact sequence of events are a little murky. But I do know that eventually the dreaded day came when it was time to leave Ohio and the warmth of that rickety little house and the family I had come to love. We were about to embark on yet another uncertain journey; one that would take us from *something* back to *nothing* again. And it happened. We said goodbye to Ohio. We were back on the road. The car had, once again, become our temporary home. I remember some scary nights spent in the car. One time in particular, we were parked for the night and in the distance we could hear what sounded like chains getting closer and closer to us. We never actually saw anything because we ended up leaving that location but I'll never forget the, almost, paralyzing fear I felt that night.

I don't know exactly when we arrived in Huntsville, AL, but suddenly, there we were. I remember how beautiful the college campus was; I'd never seen anything like it. But beauty notwithstanding, we still had nothing except each other. We were in a new place with nameless faces and unfamiliar surroundings. It was an all-too-familiar situation that forced us to, once again, rely on the kindness of strangers.

I'm not entirely sure why, but between the ages of five and eight years old, I developed an unusual fascination with birds; it was almost some kind of mystical connection. As odd as it may sound, birds would appear whenever I felt sad or fearful. Although, in hindsight, I'm not sure whether the whole thing was the result of an eight-year-old boy's overactive imagination or if it really happened. Did the birds somehow sense my pain? Could they have been sent to comfort me? I may never know for sure. But at eight years old and on the verge of what could be defined as clinical depression, I found birds to be such a source of solace and consolation, and sometimes I still do. It's something I'll never forget.

There was an elementary school on the college campus. It was a private school that required tuition to attend. And, somehow, my brothers and I were enrolled. I say "somehow" because sometimes I'm still baffled at how my father was able to accomplish that amazing feat, given the fact that money was in short supply at that time. For all intents and purposes, we were homeless. I remember a few times not being able to attend class because my tuition hadn't been paid. And on a campus where most of the students came from well-to-do families, unpaid tuition was like wearing a scarlet letter. It was embarrassing and humiliating. In addition to, occasionally, not being able to attend class, there were also times I had to endure the embarrassment of eating baby food sandwiches for lunch. It consisted of actual baby food between two slices of bread. While I was lucky to have lunch at all, I was ashamed to eat in front of the other kids who had more appetizing meals. Keep in mind that, at this school, the kids would compare and share lunches. But I wasn't a part of that because mine was never good enough to share. Eventually, my lunchtime plight caught the eye of a fellow student who was a really good kid, and from time to time he would bring extra food for me. It was a horrible predicament to be in at that age. It was difficult to weigh the pangs of hunger against the shame of being viewed as a charity case. I don't think I wanted to be pitied by my peers, but I was grateful when they did take pity on me and help me.

Bouncing around from place to place and being basically homeless is not something that can be readily understood by an eight-year-old. It's not the kind of life a young child should live. While most kids my age were playing with their friends, going to school, and then going home to warm meals and a nice warm bed at night, I was wondering where I'd sleep and where my next meal was coming from.

One of the worse times I recall, was when we took up residence in a dilapidated old trailer with no heat, no electricity and no running water. In the dead of winter, this was the only place available for us to live at that time. The trailer had, obviously, long since been abandoned and had a huge hole in the floor where frigid, bone-chilling cold poured in like gangbusters. The glacial nighttime temperatures were so brutal that we slept with all our clothes on—sandwiched between a mattress and box spring. In the morning, one of us would go out to get water from a neighbor's outdoor water spigot so we could attempt to wash up before school. But under those conditions, it wasn't possible for three kids and an adult to be fully cleansed with the small amount of cold water we hauled back from the neighbor. Added to that, was the fact that school was about a five-mile trek that we had to walk. Our living circumstances were such that I had to wear clothes that hadn't been washed in ages, and were far from clean and fresh. Sometimes the kids would move away from me holding their noses because I smelled. I was already in a fragile state of mind; bordering on depression, and now in addition to that I was a dirty little waif that other kids shunned and picked on. The continuous shame and humiliation caused me to develop low self-esteem and a poor self-image. I viewed myself as a perpetual vagabond surrounded by kids who had seemingly idyllic, storybook lives. They had nice homes to go to where their parents loved and cared for them, I didn't. Most of all, the other kids had mothers at home, I didn't. It wasn't necessarily wealth or material things that I craved, it was more a sense of security and affection from both parents that all the other kids seemed to have.

I believe that deeply embedded within the inner-sanctum of every child there's a need to be nurtured and loved by a mother and a father. It's a hunger and craving that needs to be constantly fed during the formative years. Being deprived of both <u>maternal</u> and <u>material</u> needs for long periods of time left me seriously scarred and emotionally malnourished. Not only was I emotionally hungry, I was also physically hungry. Seems like I was always in a constant state of hunger. Out of desperation, I would stand outside the school's campus store and ask for money to buy something to eat. One day, a well-known, highly-respected gentleman in the community was heading toward the store. In my little eight-year-old mind, I thought surely if anyone would give me money for food it would be this man. But I was sorely wrong. Instead of sympathizing and extending mercy and compassion to a hungry child this, supposedly, upstanding man cursed at me. I was shocked by his cruelty. He told me he wasn't giving me a dime because I had no means to pay him back. I couldn't believe how coldhearted he was. The way he responded to me when I asked for help was such a crushing blow that I never stood out there and asked for help again. Instead, I would just go hungry and hope that somehow, some way I would eat.

I had also begun to take sporadic trips back to New Jersey to spend time with my mother, but the visits were sometimes tense and strained. By then, there was such division within the family that whatever unity had existed prior to us leaving with dad had been replaced by dissension and hostility, which is nothing new in broken home situations but still hard to deal with when you're living it.

Being separated from my mother for long stretches of time made it tough for me to sense and feel the love that I now know was ever-present in her heart for me. I didn't feel a bond between us. I know she loved all of her children dearly, and that her love for us had no boundaries—its depths ran deeper than the deepest ocean. I was too young to understand that then. But later in my life I came to realize and understand that the anger and rage she harbored had nothing to do with me, it was simply her inability to suppress the bitterness and ill feelings she had at that time toward my father. In that era, it wasn't a common practice for couples and families in crisis to seek help from counselors or family therapists. You just didn't air your dirty laundry like that. In those days, seeking outside help to deal with personal problems within your household could easily be construed as weakness. Pride sometimes made it taboo in that cultural climate to invite strangers into your personal affairs. Families just dealt with their issues as best they could, regardless of what they were. More often than not, when serious conflict reared its ugly head in a family, that family unit was just doomed to fail and disintegrate. Some parents don't know how to cope with their feelings of anxiety, rejection or any number of other volatile emotions that rage when the marriage starts to deteriorate. They don't know how to extinguish flames that are fueled by anger and resentment. Some will misdirect those built-up feelings of animosity toward their children, when in reality it's not the child they're angry with at all, it's the estranged spouse. My mother was no exception to this rule. The anger that grew and festered inside of her sometimes made life stressful and uncomfortable for those around her.

Being so young at that time, it was impossible for me to come to terms with frequent homelessness, and feeling rejected and unloved by my mother. There was no explanation that anyone could have given me that I would have understood. I was far from being equipped with the wisdom and life experience that it takes to cope with hard times. I needed so much back then, and didn't understand why those needs weren't met. I needed stability; I needed my mother; I needed a brighter world around me. The absences of those things in my life were contributing factors that initially led to my depression. And depression was the catalyst that led to my downward spiral.

In those days, the term dyslexic had not yet emerged, so my learning difficulties went undiagnosed for many years. I just thought I was dumb. I would cringe whenever I thought the teacher was going to call on me to say something in class. I never wanted to get up in front of the class and be put on display for all the other kids to laugh at my ignorance. I later found out that I had suffered from dyslexia for years without knowing it. I had no idea that my inability to read and speak well was the result of a "now" common disorder. Battling a learning disability wasn't the only source of anguish that infiltrated my youth; there was something even more unspeakable that contaminated my innocence. Of all the horrible things that a child can experience, sexual molestation tops the list. It's a violation of the most basic of human rights and the damage it does to a child is inexpressible. Every person has a right to the sanctity of their own body, and a right to not be violated by anyone, ever. While we were living with one of the many families that took us in during our time on the road, I became a victim of this deplorable act. I was eight years old at the time, and this particular family's older daughter would use me for her sexual experiments and recreation. Not only was it shameful and demeaning, it was also painful. I never told my father about it because I knew if I told him, he would have taken us away from there and that would have meant living in the car again. So, I endured the degrading exploitation in silence just so we could have shelter. Putting up with it just seemed to be a better option than going back out on the road and living in the car. But no one, especially a child, can harbor that kind of shame and dehumanization without it adversely affecting them at some point in time, and in many different areas of their life. Instability alone was enough to send me plummeting into an emotional dungeon, now coupled with that was the shameful secret I had to keep for the sake of having a roof over my head. Inevitably, I began to buckle beneath the weight of all that life had dumped on me. I became withdrawn and introverted. I was slowly locking myself away in my own private little prison. An inward prison can seem as isolated and lonely as the one made of iron bars and razor wire. Sometimes your own personal prison is even more confining. You feel worthless and detached from the rest of the world as though your very existence is meaningless.

Life's highway can be bumpy and full of potholes and, unfortunately, life doesn't wait until you're old enough to handle certain things before it throws them at you. I lacked so much and lost so many things—so many vital components of my life as a young child, and with each loss came more insecurity and depression. I remember when I lost my grandmother, Josephine Anderson. She was a wonderful, God-fearing woman, and when I think of her, I'm reminded of how gentle, loving, and soft-spoken she was, and what a huge void her passing left in my life. There were times when we'd be drifting from place to place with no real home, and would show up on her doorstep in Hoboken, New Jersey. It didn't matter what time it was; sometimes it would be two, three, four o'clock in the morning. Grandma's kitchen was never closed. Whenever we showed up, she'd throw her arms open and welcome us in. She had this little saying she'd playfully say to us: "You LUV chicken?" We'd say "Yes," and she'd make chicken for us. She'd continue to ask if we loved this food or that food and whatever it was, she'd make it for us, day or night. I remember the nightgowns she wore. I can even remember the sweet fragrance that exuded from her when she squeezed me in her loving arms. Her heart's desire was that her children and grandchildren would experience the best that life could offer, and that one day the whole family would become faithful churchgoers. Dad would often tell us stories about his mother and how she would go to church even when no one else did. I remember the wonderful meals she prepared for us, and her long beautiful hair that she'd brush while sitting in her favorite chair. I believe she would have taken all of us in and raised us, but my father wanted us with him no matter what, and she respected her son's right to raise his own children. But we knew that she was there and that she loved us. We were still in Huntsville, AL when dad got word that she was gravely ill and in the hospital. I was still very young but I remember dad's sense of urgency to get to her; we had to get there quick. With the tough times we were going through, it's only by the grace and mercy of God that we were able to get back home to see her one last time. It was a cold, snowy night when we arrived. Dad rushed us out of the car and into the hospital. Grandma wasn't doing well at all, she was in a coma. Dad leaned down and began to softly speak to her. I heard him say, "Mama, I'm here, and the boys are with me." She wasn't able to respond but I've always carried the hope that she heard him. I believe she held on with every ounce of strength she had until her baby boy (my dad) and his three little boys could get there. That same night, she passed away.

Her funeral was a somber time of remembrance and as sorrowful as one would expect under the circumstances. My mother was there, and I remember her crying as we stood beside my grandma's casket. I didn't want to look at my grandma lying there—I just couldn't handle it, so I turned away. My mother turned my head back toward my grandma and I quickly turned away again and buried my face in my mother's stomach. It was an indescribable pain to see my beloved grandmother lying there lifeless. Her arms had been the safest place in my world, and she was gone. She couldn't hug me anymore; she couldn't tell me she loved me anymore; there would never be another home-cooked meal from grandma's kitchen. I didn't know how to act, or what to say or how to feel. I thought she'd always be there; thought I'd always have the safety and comfort of her arms. She never ran out of love and I'll always miss her. After her funeral we headed back to Alabama.

I'm sure we've all heard quotes and read greeting cards that express warm thoughts and sweet little anecdotes about grandparents, in general. But it's difficult to adequately articulate what "your" very own grandmother means, or meant, to you. In 1971, a very gifted man by the name of Bill Withers recorded an amazing song that conveyed what his grandmother meant to him. You may or may not be familiar with the song but the sentiment behind the lyrics is hard to miss. It's one of those heart-warming songs that we can never have too many of.

The song was called *Grandma's hands* and the lyrics went like this:

Grandma's hands
Clapped in church on Sunday morning
Grandma's hands
Played the tambourine so well
Grandma's hands
Used to issue out a warning

BEAUTIFUL SCARS

She'd say, "Billy don't you run so fast
Might fall on a piece of glass
"Might be snakes there in that grass"
Grandma's hands

Grandma's hands
Soothed a local unwed mother
Grandma's hands
Used to ache sometimes and swell
Grandma's hands
Used to lift her face and tell her,
She'd say, "Baby, Grandma understands
That you really love that man
Put yourself in Jesus' hands"
Grandma's hands

Grandma's hands
Used to hand me a piece of candy
Grandma's hands
Picked me up each time I fell
Grandma's hands
Boy, they really came in handy
She'd say, "Matty don't you whip that boy
What you want to spank him for?
He didn't drop no apple core"
But I don't have Grandma anymore
If I get to Heaven I'll look for
Grandma's hands

Mr. Withers put to music what lives in the hearts of so
many of us who were blessed with the love of a
grandmother.

A garden of Love grows in a Grandmother's heart.
- Author Unknown

Grandma's heart is a Patchwork of Love.
- Author Unknown

Grandmother-grandchild relationships are simple. Grandmas
are short on criticism and long on love.
- Author Unknown

Grandmothers and roses are much the same, each are God's
masterpieces with different names.
- Author Unknown

CHAPTER TWO

My dad had completed his studies and received his theology degree by the time I finished ninth grade. A short time later he became a full time minister. My parents had officially divorced, and dad eventually remarried. He and my stepmother gave me two beautiful little sisters who became my pride and joy. Blended families, in general, can be challenging, to say the least, and a minister's family is not exempt from the same conflict and friction that exists in non-religious families. At that time, I didn't really know anything about household etiquette or the proper way to do things—I had more or less lived a transient-type lifestyle. My stepmother tried to make a nice home for us but I didn't have the social skills or behavioral wherewithal to properly integrate myself into this nice clean house. I hadn't attended Miss Manners' classes or fancy Finishing Schools that teach you all about social grace and etiquette. It wasn't that I didn't appreciate her and her efforts, I genuinely did. I just simply didn't

21

know how to conduct myself in that type of stable environment. It had been much too long since I'd been in a stable home and it was difficult for me to acclimate. Early on, this caused understandable conflict in the home.

Dad's first ministry appointment was in Gastonia, North Carolina. For most families (at least families that society views as "normal"), a move to a new place is often an exciting time—filled with anticipation for a new beginning with new hope and expectations of a brighter future. But a geographical change did nothing to end my accelerating downward spiral. I was still sinking deeper into depression. And by then, my depression had begun to manifest itself outwardly. I developed a severe case of acne; so severe that I couldn't bear to look at myself in the mirror. While it's possible to mask inner-pain beneath a camouflage of fake laughter or counterfeit contentment, it's not so easy to hide the clearly visible scars that show outwardly; the ones that you believe nullify your worth and value as a human being. I couldn't conceal the horrible blemishes that covered my face and made me feel as ugly outside as I felt inside. And so, the more depressed I became, the more the acne worsened, and the more the acne worsened the more depressed I became. I was caught up and entangled in a vicious circle. Some would say, there's nothing uncommon about teenagers experiencing bouts with acne, and most deal with it as part of growing up. But for me, it was just one more thing to add to my already low opinion of myself. I thought so little of myself and was so repulsed by my severely scarred face that I, literally, wanted to disappear.

In eleventh grade, I was sent to a Christian boarding school in Pottstown, PA. By then, I wasn't a boy anymore I was a young man, but still lugging around the same insecurities and poor self-image I'd had pretty much all my life. Again, I was surrounded by kids who <u>had</u> and I was still one of the <u>have-nots</u>. But there was a unique difference at this school; this time I was able to form friendships and connect with some of the kids who had come there from various places around the east coast. Many of them had life experiences similar to mine, and had gone through some tough times as well. So, I was able to establish a bond and sense of camaraderie that I hadn't been able to develop before. I connected with them in a way that I hadn't connected with kids at my other schools. But little did I know that our common-ground was littered with landmines and sinkholes. We were teetering on the edge of a bottomless pit of darkness and none of us saw it coming. It was during my junior year that I was introduced to alcohol and marijuana. I had never experienced it before, but I remember being stunned by an instant feeling of euphoria; I was suddenly pain-free. I'd been hurting inside for so long that it was like jubilation to find a substance that actually dulled the pain. My friends and I habitually drank alcohol and smoked marijuana right there on school property. You wouldn't expect something like drug and alcohol use to occur in a religious learning institution where parents expected their children to be hovered over, protected and taught good wholesome values. But it happened. And, in fact, there was a teacher there who was part of the problem rather than the solution. This teacher would smoke marijuana and get high with us at school. It's a shocking realization that this could happen in a Christian-based learning environment. But, sadly, it's probably not that uncommon. Troubled kids often become troubled adults—irrespective of the external environment. My friends and I didn't have the mental and emotional fortitude to know that we were on a path to destruction. Even more troubling, is the fact that sometimes adults in positions of authority contribute to kids' wayward behavior, which was the case with us and the teacher.

The pathway of a child with no direction, no self-value and no realistic expectations of a bright, successful future is all-too-predictable. Far too many young people find themselves between a rock and a hard place just as I did; wanting so badly to fit in and be accepted by my peers and homies from the hood. You want to be part of the crew. But also, deep down inside there's another yearning trying to tunnel its way to the surface. Underneath all the muck and mire there lies a genuine desire for something more out of life— something other than the cloudiness of despair and substance dependency. When you descend into the world of drugs and alcohol, you may convince yourself that that's the life you want to live. But the desire to be free, the desire for something better never goes away. I was no exception. I was becoming dependent on the substances to make me feel good about myself. The tug of war between good and evil is a fierce one, even for a Minister's son. No matter how hard I tried to free myself I always returned to the familiarity of the streets and everything that came with them. I had become a slave to drugs and alcohol. My ever-progressing addiction ruled me. So much so, that when no alcohol was available, my friends and I would drink Nyquil. It didn't matter what the substance was as long as it was something that would take me from reality and put me in an altered state. I just couldn't handle being myself in the real world.

Surprisingly, I managed to graduate from high school, and I was ecstatic that my mother attended my graduation. After being away from her for so much of my life, I was pretty happy when she asked me to go back to New Jersey with her. I chose to go because it was an opportunity to get to know her better. I really didn't know my mother very well at all and I needed to know her. It seemed like a good choice at the time, but it turned out to be a huge mistake. Jersey wasn't the same place it was when I lived there as a five-year-old child. The streets were scary and drugs were plentiful. It was after I moved back with my mother that I became acquainted with harder drugs, such as cocaine. I used cocaine incessantly, and in a variety of forms from crack cocaine to powdered. But even in the midst of all the chaos in my life, I became very particular about my appearance. I managed to get jobs and was always well-dressed and groomed. Being neat and clean had become a new obsession of mine since I had grown up feeling like I was dirty all the time. Prior to my descent into serious drug addiction, I used most of my money to buy nice clothes. But as my addiction progressed and intensified, there were times when my entire paycheck would be spent on cocaine. Drugs were in abundant supply, and if that wasn't bad enough, I could freely use drugs on my job. My boss and I bought drugs from the same dealer. It was very easy for me to freely destroy myself.

As in every case of chronic drug addiction, when the drugs wear off the depression and anxiety come back in full force with a vengeance. When I wasn't high on something, I would plunge so deep into depression that I couldn't wait to be high again. Somewhere deep within the recesses of my spirit I knew it wasn't the life I should have been living, but I was being controlled by a force more powerful than I. And I was powerless to stop. Before long my addiction caused conflict between me and my mother. There was bound to be a certain amount of tension between us anyway given the fact that we hardly knew each other. I had gone away an innocent child but returned a drug-addicted young man. And so, day by day our relationship gradually began to sour. At the height of the conflict, I moved in with a co-worker and his parents in Orange, New Jersey. I'll never forget Mr. Willie Thomas and his wife Mrs. Sandra Thomas. I have such fond memories of living in their beautiful home and how nice they were to me. They charged me a minuscule amount to stay there, and advised me to put the rest of my money away for college. Back then, I was incapable of fully appreciating the magnitude of their kindness and what this family was doing for me. I couldn't see beyond what I had become. There came a point in time that out of concern for my survival, my mother took a bold step and told the Thomases about my drug use, which they weren't aware of. Not long afterwards, I moved out... more for their sake than mine.

Oddly enough, in all the chaos and turmoil in my life, I still miraculously manage to go to college for a while though finances were always an issue. I would sometimes hide in a friend's dorm room when I had no place else to go. Those times were reminiscent of the times as a child I had slept on dorm room floors when my father was attending theology school in Alabama. Seemed as if no matter what I did something always conjured up memories of the past; it was always coming back to haunt me. Everyday life served as a constant reminder that there was no hope for me... at least, that's how I felt. Around every corner was the harsh reality of nothingness.

You can't live the kind of life I was living and not have brushes with the law—it's just inevitable. And I had my share of run-ins with law-enforcement. On one occasion, a friend and I had just purchased some drugs and were pulled over by the police. We had just left a pretty hardcore spot; an abandoned building in N.Y. where men yielding guns guarded the drug stash. I was sweating and scrambling trying to hide the drugs in the crevices of the car. I was able to successfully wiggle my way out of arrest that day. But eventually my luck ran out and I was arrested and spent time in jail on drug-related charges. As I continued to spiral out-of-control, I stopped caring about right and wrong. I would do whatever was necessary; beg, borrow or steal to feed an addiction that I had not yet come to realize was the by-product of years of depression. Staying high was the only way I could drive the depression out. The drugs had taken center stage in my life and I was obedient to them. Since I had developed a reputation for being meticulous about how I dressed, people really took notice when my appearance began to change. I still had very bad acne but, in spite of that, I had always dressed to impress. And when that changed, it was really glaring and noticeable to everyone who knew me. I stopped caring about how I looked. I descended even deeper into an abyss of anguish, hopelessness and despair. It was to the point where I felt like giving up on life. And, in fact, there came a time when I did give up. I wanted out. I saw no reason to go on living. The loosely woven fabric of my life was unraveling. I made the decision to end my life, and methodically planned how I would do it. I didn't want a painful death because I had already suffered enough pain. I wanted a painless, peaceful departure from the world. So, that fateful day, when I got my paycheck, I bought an assortment of drugs; anything and everything I could get my hands on. I began ingesting them in rapid succession knowing that eventually I would take enough to end my life. After I had taken what I thought was more than enough to finish the job, I waited for death in silent resolve. I was in such a deep hole that I wanted to be sure and die in the darkness of night because I didn't want to see another sunrise. At some point, I drifted into unconsciousness. But at the crack of dawn, surprisingly, I was still alive and not at all happy about it. I was disappointed that I had survived the night. I felt as though my own body had betrayed me. Having been raised a God-fearing person, one of the first thoughts that crept in through my drug-induced haze, was the fear of losing my soul if I took my own life. So there I was—still living, and a brutal storm with no mercy was raging inside of me. I was sweating profusely, vomiting, stumbling around, staggering and falling down. All the while a still small voice within was telling me to call my dad. I wanted my dad to pray for me. Maybe I wanted his prayers for my soul just in case I ended up dying after all, I don't know. But I knew I had to reach him. I felt as though God would listen to him because he was a minister. I didn't think God would listen to me because of the mess my life was. I needed my father's prayers. I staggered to a payphone. At that time, dad was down in South Carolina. I called him and he prayed for me. He told me to hold on. Dad called my aunt, who lived near the city I was in and she came and took me to the hospital. Looking back, I can only imagine how horrible that must have been for my father being in another state and hearing his son on the other end of the phone in that condition; not knowing if I'd live or die.

I woke up in the hospital, alive but in a fog. It felt like I was outside of my body. I could hear my uncle's voice and other voices and hospital noises going on around me, but I didn't feel as though I was a part of anything that was happening. It was like being in a parallel universe where you're observing yourself from the outside, and you're aware of others but they're not aware of you. The fact that I was still alive didn't automatically mean that all was well. Surviving the overdose hadn't ended my depression. I was still just as miserable—maybe even more so. After my release from the hospital, dad came to get me and took me back with him to South Carolina. Once I was there with him, I tried to clean up my life. I even started going to Church again. For a while I was headed in the right direction. But then I found myself in the same tug of war again battling against good and evil, right and wrong, and I was losing the battle. I started gravitating toward the dark side again. I still hadn't conquered the gloom and hopelessness inside of me. I started looking for drugs and people to do drugs with. It didn't take long to find them. Once again, there I was back in that same gloomy abyss I'd been clawing tooth and nail to escape from.

I've been told that I was blessed with a beautiful voice, and I've always loved to sing. As a child, I would sing to my father to keep him awake on the road when we were traveling from place to place. Singing was second nature for me; it's therapeutic, soothing and uplifting. So, eventually I formed a singing group. We were initially pretty successful securing gigs at various nightclubs around town. Music being the beautiful art it is, I suppose I could have latched on to it and used it as a deterrent from my addiction since many have found that immersing oneself in music can sometimes be a positive distraction from destructive vices. But it couldn't work for me back then because the clubs we played in were full of drug addicts and dealers. In that environment it was impossible for me to elevate myself and rise above the temptation to continue the addictive behavior I'd become so accustomed to. Even though singing was (and still is) a great passion of mine, the addiction had a much stronger hold on me. And in an atmosphere fraught with self-destruction and people who condoned and encouraged drug use, it was so easy for me to return to my old ways. As a Minister's son, I had a firm, biblically-based foundation. But still the adversarial war inside of me raged on; light versus darkness, right versus wrong, good versus evil, and the adversary was winning. I was still engulfed in depression, not even recognizing it for what it was. I lived a life that was vile, depraved and shameful. My conscience switch was stuck in the <u>off</u> position. My moral compass was broken.

I was put on probation for one year after being arrested but that didn't really phase me. I had reached a point where nothing mattered to me—not even the people I loved who also loved me. I would sell or pawn my family's belongings to get money for drugs. I even went so far as to ride around looking for some unsuspecting person to rob. Violence was never a part of my character, and the act of robbing an innocent person was something I would ordinarily have never dreamed of doing if not for the addiction that took control of my life. Thankfully, I never actually did it but the temptation was there. There came a time when I didn't even know myself. I lost all touch with reality. The depression coupled with the substance abuse rendered me incapable of realizing that I was loved, and that there was hope beyond the pit of despair. There was light beyond the darkness that encapsulated me. There was healing on the other side of all the pain.

CHAPTER THREE

Anyone who has gone through or still struggles with the up and down cycle of depression and drug addiction knows what a lonely, empty existence it is. You need to escape so you gravitate toward a source of escapism. Drugs and alcohol provided an escape route from reality. But that momentary escape came at a very high price. It was costly in more ways than one. When the drugs wore off, I'd be even more depressed and more disgusted with the hollow shell of a person I had become. Yet, I couldn't comprehend or perceive the hurt I was inflicting on those who loved me. I didn't feel their love because I didn't feel worthy of being loved. A beautiful young lady who was a classmate of mine once told me that 'if I could only see myself the way others see me, I'd learn to love myself.' But I didn't love myself so I couldn't fathom anyone else loving me. I did everything I could to escape the reality of just being. Existing everyday was an agonizing struggle that I know so many people can relate to. Drugs helped me separate from the self I loathed. I wasn't really living I was just breathing in and out.

On the home front, I caused one chaotic incident after another. I just didn't care about anything or anyone. I wrecked my father's car one night on the way to the club and I really don't even have a clear recollection of what actually happened. I do remember being at the club and noticing that the car was wrecked and having no memory of how it happened.

On a separate occasion, I went so far as to sell my father's car while he was out of town. I had no regard for the rights and property of others, not even my own family. I couldn't see anything beyond my next high. I even tried selling drugs myself for a short time but I was using more than I sold, which made my drug-dealing enterprise futile. So, I had to constantly stay in the company of other dealers who were able to keep the portal open and continuously funnel drugs to me.

The one positive thing I did consistently was get jobs. Somehow, I could always manage to find work. But my willingness to work was always overshadowed by my ultimate goal, which, obviously, was to be able to finance my substance use.

As an addict, I couldn't be a healthy component of the family even though, sometimes, I really wanted to be. I wasn't mentally or emotionally capable of valuing and accepting my family's concern and the constant prayers they sent up for me. I lived in the shadow of death; everything around me was dark. And as time went on it got even darker. No one else understood what I was going through, but then... neither did I. All I knew is that I was chained and bound. Only someone who's been through it can understand the inner-torment of it all. I hated my addiction and hated myself because of the addiction. I hated the way I looked on the outside, and hated the way I felt on the inside.

People will be people, and most don't mind sharing their criticisms about *your* family and life situations. Being true to their human nature, people started voicing their opinions about what they thought my father should do with me. The vast majority said they'd never put up with a drug-addicted child who was doing the things I was doing. But for those who aren't living in the midst of the storm, who aren't watching their child slowly and methodically destroy himself, but are only on the outside looking in, it's easy to say what they would or wouldn't do in the same situation. It's easy to presume what you'd do if faced with the same set of circumstances. But it's only a presumption because no one can ever really know until they are faced with it and have to live it themselves. My father continually showed his love for me and refused to give up on me no matter how many times I gave up on myself.

One of the greatest displays of my father's love for me was the day he boldly spoke to his whole congregation. He addressed all the people who had been badmouthing me and saying they'd put their child out or do this or that if it was their son behaving like I was behaving. Several people had told my father that if it was their son they'd put him in a mental institution or throw him out on the street. On that particular Sabbath, I was sitting at the back of the church with my head down, feeling empty and broken inside like I always did. But I can still remember my father's exact words as he stood there at the podium. He said:

"I want to address those of you who have called to tell me what you'd do if it was your son doing these things. Well, if it was your son I probably would put him out or in a mental institution. But this is my son. I don't understand what he's going through but I'm going to stick by him no matter what."

Up to that point I had doubted my father's love for me; I doubted everyone's love for me. But as I sat there that day with tears cascading down my face, I realized what an amazing man my father was and how much he really did love me. I wish his love had been enough to fix my life and make everything right. But it wasn't. I still had to deal with "me" inside.

I'm sure people wondered (and continue to wonder), why someone with a loving family would continue down the path I was on. But being loved by others isn't always enough. Before you can fully value and receive love from others, you have to learn to love yourself. Only then can you begin to heal and overcome deep-rooted anxiety and depression. I didn't understand that I had an illness; I just knew I felt empty, hopeless and hated myself. I had no idea I was suffering from clinical depression. And without a proper diagnosis you can't be treated. It's easy for others to criticize and say what they'd do, but no one knows the depth of the pain except the one who's hurting.

> *"The greatest freedom or prison that the mind could have is your belief"*

CHAPTER FOUR

Dad was called to a new ministry appointment in Goldsboro, and although I could have gone with him, I didn't because I didn't feel I was ready to go to a new place. At that time, I didn't see any point in moving.

As tumultuous as my life was while my dad was in town with me, it was nothing compared to the tailspin I went into after he left and I was no longer under his watchful eye. Life quickly went from bad to worse; things got worse than they had ever been for me. I drifted around from place to place. I had been a pretty stout guy, but not long after dad left town I became frail and sickly-looking. I was dirty, smelly and walked around in a perpetual groggy daze—sleeping wherever I could. There was a certain woman who had taken a liking to me and allowed me to stay with her in exchange for sexual favors.   And I had sunk low enough to take her up on the offer just to have a place to stay. When that got old, I stayed wherever and with whomever I could until I realized things weren't getting better they were only getting worse.

Before dad left town, he gave a set of car keys (for a car he left behind) to a fellow-pastor friend and asked that the keys be given to me as soon as I expressed a desire to join my father in Goldsboro. Dad told his friend to give me the keys and send me his way as soon as I was ready to go. After many turbulent months on the street, the day came when I was ready to go where my dad was. I knew I had to do something so I headed for Goldsboro. I had never been there before so I didn't know anything about the layout of the city or where anything was. All I had was an address. I don't remember much about my drive there, that part has always been pretty cloudy in my mind. But I do remember it was a hot summer day when I ended up outside my dad's home. To this day, I label my arrival as a sovereign act of the Almighty Creator because that's the only way I could have arrived there safely. No one was home when I got there and I remember feeling so exhausted my body just gave out. When the family got home they found me passed out in the seat with all the windows down. I was sweaty and disoriented, and they took me inside. I know they were as perplexed as I was that I even made it there in one piece, considering the condition I was in.

So there I was in a new city with another chance for a new beginning. But it was easy to see that joining my family in North Carolina didn't automatically signal a change in my lifestyle. It was only a change of location. I brought the same old baggage with me; it was impossible to escape myself. No matter where I went, there I was—still dragging around the ball and chain of my addiction. And pretty soon, predictably like clockwork, just as it had always been, I started searching for the drug zone. And as usual, I found it.

For reasons I don't fully understand, I was always somewhat of a woman-magnet. On the surface this might seem like a good thing. But I, unfortunately, seemed to frequently attract the wrong kind. It's typical to migrate toward the wrong kind of people when you're in a weakened, self-destructive state of mind because misery loves company and wrong begets wrong. Before long, I became acquainted with a young woman who had the "hook-up" so to speak, and she directed me straight to the drug district. For many people I'm sure it's baffling as to how someone with a family support-system fully intact like mine could continually and blindly navigate into deadly waters. But, as I said earlier, it's not always about your family status. It's not always about the environment you live in. It's not always about what's going on around you, it's more about what's going on inside of you. That's one of the things that so many people have such difficulty understanding. Once again, unless you've lived it, it's not easy to fully comprehend being driven to destruction and powerless to stop it.

I was causing such a disruption in the peace and harmony of my father's home that I soon returned to my transient lifestyle. I was back to living in abandoned houses, staying in crack houses, and hooking up with dangerous people. I was always broke, so I started getting drugs on the "pay later" plan, which in and of itself is risky business. Owing money for drugs is a dangerous state of affairs, and I owed money to dealers who didn't believe in charity, and had no qualms about hurting people. One night in a crack house, I found myself on the receiving end of at least eight guys out to teach me a lesson about paying my drug debt. They started beating me unmercifully, and I was incapable of defending myself against all of them. It's only by the grace of God that I managed to somehow push my way through them and escape with my life. But the beating still wasn't enough to make me stop, I just found a different dealer.

After my first hospitalization, I was put on various medications, but what I didn't know then was that unless you learn coping skills and techniques that go beyond medicating, you'll fall right back into the same hole. And that's exactly what happened. Depression, once again, got the better of me and I attempted suicide a second time. This time was far more sinister than the first time. I was back living with my dad, he was out of town and the rest of the family wasn't home at that time. I had sold quite a few of their belongings, and taken the money dad kept in the house and combined it with the money I had so I could purchase an arsenal of drugs. I promised myself I'd do it right this time. This time would be the finale. I was done with life. I was tired. I just didn't want to go on anymore. I was in my room with a crack pipe and what I thought was enough crack cocaine to end it all, for once and for all. I started taking hits off the pipe, and as I smoked it I began to feel as though I was being watched. Crack cocaine has a tendency to make you paranoid anyway, and the amount I was smoking made the paranoia even more intense. I was convinced I was being watched. But I didn't care about anything except making my heart stop. I remember actually hitting the pipe so hard that night that I <u>did</u> feel my heart stop. And judging by the way my body started to feel, I knew this time was going to work. I felt myself leaving; like life was draining out of my body. At that point I took the biggest, longest hit off the pipe that I could. I knew I would soon ingest enough smoke to cause my heart to explode. I still felt the paranoia though. I was still certain that someone was watching me. I went over to my bedroom window and looked outside, and as plain as anything I saw two demons sitting on the roof of the house across the street. There were two figures black from head to toe with fire-red eyes sitting on the roof smoking. I could see smoke just billowing out of both their mouths. After I saw them I jumped back so hard I fell against the bedroom wall. And when I mustered the courage to look out again, they were still there looking back at me. They were as real as anything I'd ever seen. My heart was racing, sweat was pouring off me, and I'd never felt such panic and terror before. When I looked out again these two black figures, that I will always refer to as demons, started floating through the air toward me and landed on our front lawn. I could literally hear them walking. I watched them walk across the lawn and hide behind a tree. They would peek out at me from behind the tree, like they were taunting and mocking me. By this time I was going into some kind of catatonic state. I had ripped all of my clothes off and was completely naked. These demons teased and poked fun at me to the point that I wasn't scared anymore, I was mad. I went charging outside and stood on the porch challenging them to come and get me. I went berserk. There I was, outside on the front porch—stark naked, pacing up and down yelling and shouting to the top of my lungs at these demons. I was screaming: "Come and get me. I'm not goin' out like a punk, come and get me." I'm still amazed that no one called the police on me, considering what a nice quiet neighborhood this was. And I'm sure countless people heard me ranting and raving. After I went back inside, I hit the floor and started crying. I sobbed like a baby, all the while asking God to forgive me. I cried until I passed out on the floor. I woke up the next morning in the same spot; naked and cold with body-fluids everywhere. The Creator in His infinite mercy had spared my life again.

Brian Keith Anderson

It was after that second suicide attempt that I wrote this poem to God:

This battle that I fight seems oh so hard to win
My life is so confused my soul all filled with sin
When burdens get me down I turn to GOD in prayer
Still wondering if He cares or if He's even there
I strayed so far from YOU my faith was almost gone
Then YOU stretched out your hand
And cried "My child hold on."

Forgive me, Lord, forgive me!
Forgive me, Lord, forgive me!

He left His Father's side a fight He had to win
Often getting tired but never giving in
Some laughed some called Him names
Some said He's not the one
The people often said, the Savior's yet to come
They marched Him up that hill my cross He had to bare
They crucified my Lord, Heaven knows it wasn't fair.

Forgive me, Lord, forgive me!
Forgive me, Lord, forgive me!

He came, He bled, He died, my Lord was crucified
High atop Golgotha's hill He cried, "Not my will."
I hear the rush of wings I hear the angels sing
Behold the King of Kings say, "Death where is your sting?"

Lord here I stand alone, my faith is not that strong
Still wanting to come home that's why I sing this song

Forgive me, Lord, forgive me!
Forgive me, Lord, forgive me!

***

Frederick Douglass once said, "*I prayed for twenty years but received no answer until I prayed with my legs.*"

Sometimes being brought to your knees is what brings about a change. Others can pray for you and kneel on your behalf, but nothing brings about the change that hitting your own knees does.

"Faith makes things possible, not easy."

CHAPTER FIVE

I approached what would become a turning point in my life while working at a mental health/group home facility. Unfortunately, once again, I went into that job with my same old ways and behavior. I would steal from petty cash, smoke crack and get high at work. I was so brazen with it that one day after I had come out of the bathroom a patient came up to me and said, "You been smokin' crack! Look at you! You been smokin' crack!" I knew then and there if it was that obvious to patients, sooner or later it was going to be obvious to my boss. But I didn't stop.

It was at this job that I met a man named Curtis Gram. Curtis was the kind of person everyone wanted to be around. He seemed to have it all together and everybody loved him. I didn't realize what a positive, motivating force he would become in my life. I always assumed his life was perfect. He had a beautiful family, he was upbeat and cheerful all the time, it just seemed as though he had never had a care in the world. But I found out that his life hadn't been perfect. As things on the job started to deteriorate with me, he came to me one day and said: "Listen, man, I know what you're going through." I asked him how he could possibly know what I was going through, his life was perfect. As we walked off by ourselves, he began to tell me the story of his own recovery. That was a monumental, eye-opening experience for me. Curtis was the first person I had ever known who knew exactly what I was going through. He had been there and made it to the other side. He had overcome. He had won the battle. At that moment, I realized there might be hope for me too. But my journey was going to be a long one. I know my family's prayers kept me alive, but I believe Curtis was the one who gave me hope that I could be whole and free. Curtis took me under his wing. He introduced me to his family and would take me to church with them. When I'd find myself sinking he would encourage me.

I was still using drugs and getting high at work, and one day my boss confronted me. He said he knew I was stealing and doing drugs, and he gave me an ultimatum. I had to get help or go to jail. I told my dad I needed to get to this particular treatment facility that was about two hours away. At that time dad was in the middle of a meeting of some kind and couldn't get away to take me. I was overwhelmed when Curtis stepped up and offered to drive me there. It was becoming clear to me what a blessing this man was in my life. He unselfishly donated his own time to me. I spent almost the entire trip crying. I was just so immersed in pain; everything within me was hurting, and all I could do was cry. The truly remarkable thing was that during the trip, as I cried, Curtis cried with me. It seemed as if my pain was familiar to him; maybe it brought back memories of his own. He told me that I would be okay. I couldn't remember ever being okay before. But Curtis made me think about what it would be like to really be okay—to be content with myself. This man was truly a God-send.

When I first arrived at the treatment facility, I didn't want to participate in anything. I didn't want any part of that whole rehabilitation process that I was supposed to undergo. All I wanted to do was continue my womanizing ways with all the female patients, do my time, and get out of there. I wasn't serious about it or into it at all—at least, not at first. But then one day I decided I may as well make the best of it. During a session with the staff doctor, he told me I was suffering from depression. I couldn't believe it. I thought, how could I (a big, strong black man) be depressed? But on the other hand I felt a sense of relief to know that what I had been feeling all these years had a name. It wasn't just some imaginary thing that I dreamed up. It was a real condition that a doctor diagnosed. It was an illness; a mental illness. The term "mental illness" has a historical stigma attached to it that leads some people to believe that when you've been diagnosed with a mental illness it means you're crazy or psychotic, and someone to be shunned and avoided. But society at large fails to realize that just as the body can become ill from internal and external imbalances, so can the mind. I was deprived of the emotional nutrients I needed as a child to be mentally healthy and so I grew up mentally and emotionally deficient. As Frederick Douglass said: *"It's easier to build strong children than to repair broken ones."*

The treatment facility had a lot of different activities, and one in particular was family day. This was a time for patients' family members to come and participate in group sessions. Everyone had family members there that day but my dad couldn't make it. I was the only one who didn't have a family member there. I remember looking out the window and crying because it reminded me of the times as a child when we were living in certain places I'd be so afraid sometimes, and anxious to see dad's car pull up. That same fear and loneliness was as fresh as if it had just happened. Some things are very difficult to permanently suppress.

On this particular family day, there was a man who had come there for a family member who was a patient. I had never seen or met him before. He realized that there was no family member there for me and he offered to be my surrogate father for the day. I'll never forget him—he bore a striking resemblance to Kenny Rogers. But that's not the only reason I won't forget him. The main reason is because of his kindness and the difference he made in my life that day. Our paths may never cross again but I'll always hold fond memories of the man who stood-in as my father on a day when I felt so alone. When people like that cross your path, when you receive unexpected kindness it moves you to believe there's hope for mankind. And it motivates you to want to do the same for others.

As Dr. Martin Luther King once said:

"If I can help somebody as I travel on; if I can cheer somebody with a word or a song; if I can show somebody he's traveling wrong, then my living will not be in vain. If I can do my duty as a Christian ought; if I can show salvation to a world once wrought; if I can spread the word as the Master taught, then my living will not be in vain."

CHAPTER SIX

After completing my treatment, I was eager to get on the road to recovery and start living as normal a life as I possibly could. I committed myself to getting clean. The concept of living a drug-free, "normal" life was incomprehensible to me. It was something I had never experienced in my entire adult life. I desperately wanted to know what that was like. I followed the prescribed plan the treatment facility established for me and took my medication as instructed. I was diligent in my recovery efforts even after I was released. I faithfully kept my after-care appointments and began taking herbs that my dad started me on. Dad never liked the idea of over-medicating with prescription drugs and he was familiar with certain types of herbs that I could take instead of the medication. And I believe the herbs did actually work for me. I started feeling as though I could make a go of being a whole person. That's not to say that herbs are the answer for everyone. By no means should a person disregard the benefit of well-prescribed medication. I'm just saying they worked for me, personally.

I had kept in contact with Curtis while I was in treatment, and it was with his help that I was able to completely commit to getting better. Curtis was, and still is, a great example of someone who walked in my shoes, who traveled the same road I traveled and made it through. He embodies an ideology that what you do does not define who you are and who you can become. He told me things I had never heard before. I was steeped in self-hatred most of my life. I can hardly remember a time when I walked with my head held high because I never thought much of myself. I lived with the belief that I was repulsive. I had dealt with depression, drug-abuse, horrible acne and the resultant scars—both inside and out. In my mind, I was a pathetic creature. But then Curtis Gram told me one day to say these word: *"I am somebody, I love myself, there's no one better than me."* He told me to repeat them everyday over and over until they were ingrained and cemented into my mind and into my very being. I thought it was nonsense, but I did it. I took his advice to heart and started repeating those words everyday. Everyday I said, *"I am somebody, I love myself, there's no one better than me."* It didn't happen overnight but after a while, sure enough, it started sinking in. I began to feel better about myself. I walked differently; I didn't walk with my head down anymore, I held my head high. I talked differently; I spoke with more confidence than I ever had before. It was amazing; I actually started feeling better about myself. It's important to feel good about yourself because YOU are the one you'll live with every minute—every second. You can't escape yourself no matter how hard you try. Curtis taught me that feeling good about oneself has nothing to do with arrogance or being self-centered or absorbed, it's about being able to look at yourself in the mirror and know that you're a human being who's just as deserving of happiness, love and respect as any other person on the face of the earth.

The simple act of being someone's friend can improve their mental health functioning.

I was glad to be able to return to my job after completing my treatment, but deep down I knew I couldn't stay in that town anymore. I wanted, and needed, a change—a fresh new start in a new place. My plan was to, ultimately, move to Augusta, Georgia, where my mother had moved years earlier to be closer to her family. I wanted to try and re-capture some of those lost years with her. When it came to my mother, I still felt like a little boy. Leading authorities in the mental health field say that it's very common for people to regress back to the time where they first disconnected from a person or event. I hadn't gone through the progressive stages of life with my mother, so inside I still felt like a sheepish child.

My mother had remarried at one point but, unfortunately, she married an abusive man. I remember an earlier incident where I witnessed him beating her. For some reason, I just froze. I guess I didn't feel capable of protecting her. So, I ran and got my brother and he stopped my stepfather from hitting her. I suppose one of the main reasons I wanted to be in Georgia was so that I could have the opportunity to step up and be my mother's protector, and care for her as her health was starting to decline. I eventually left North Carolina in pursuit of that fresh new start, and spent about six months in Alabama with my brother before finally heading to Georgia. I initially moved to Atlanta and stayed with a friend for a while, but I had to quickly get myself established because he was in the process of moving.

Suffice it to say, like any red-blooded young man, I yearned for a meaningful relationship. I believe The CREATOR embedded the desire for companionship in every human being. I wanted a wife and children of my own. The main reason I wanted children was so that I could give them all the things I missed out on when I was a child. I suppose there might have been a small part of me that wanted to, basically, re-live my own childhood through my children and somehow right all the wrongs that happened in my life. But it wasn't meant to be at that time. To everything there is a season and a time for every purpose under heaven.

After living in Atlanta about three months, I met and fell in love with a beautiful young woman who was the daughter of a prominent man in the community. Even though I was still battling some lingering inward turmoil, we got married a short time later. But our union was ill-fated from the word go because I was not yet in a good place emotionally. I hadn't learned how to fully give and accept love because I hadn't yet reached the point where I could truly love myself. I couldn't handle or accept the adoration of my young wife because I didn't feel worthy of her. And I couldn't imagine someone like her loving someone like me. I was better, but I wasn't there yet. We don't see things as they are, we see things as **WE** are. And so I allowed my own fears and issues to cause me to withdraw and throw up walls. I was unfaithful and disloyal because I was completely ill-equipped to be a positive, reciprocal partner in the marriage. It was a critical point in my recovery and I didn't realize just how critical a time it was. I was fresh out of in-patient treatment and still needing to adjust to living a drug-free adult life. I should have taken more time to get to know myself better, and find the rest of me—who I was, where I was, and what I wanted to be. It was much too soon for me to attempt a marriage because I still wasn't emotionally able to be a devoted husband. I hadn't seen the world through drug-free eyes since early in my teens. I had no idea what real life was about. All I had known before was darkness, sorrow, depression and drugs. You can't take shortcuts and look for exit signs on the road to recovery because it can be a long journey to find a place where you finally feel complete. I hadn't reached that high point in my recovery yet. So, the marriage failed. I had nothing to give, so I walked away. I figured if I didn't leave her she would leave me. It just always seemed easier and less painful to be the one who leaves rather than the one who's left.

My mother was living in Augusta at that time and had become gravely ill. When she called and told me how ill she was, I literally dropped everything and made plans to move to Augusta to take care of her. On a funny side note, the mental picture I had of Augusta was of a "Mayberry" kind of town where the deputy had one bullet that he kept in his shirt pocket. I never imagined it to be the thriving metropolis that it is. But quite frankly, I really wasn't too concerned about the look or stats of the city, I just wanted to take care of my mother no matter where she was. Shortly after I arrived in Augusta, I found a job in a mental health facility. Being in recovery myself, I tended to gravitate toward jobs in that field; it's where I felt I belonged and could do the most good.

Not long after moving to Augusta, I met another woman, moved in with her and, eventually, tried marriage again. I might have thought this time would be different, but this arrangement was fraught with new difficulties from the very beginning. This time it was more about me trying to juggle two important women in my life, and neither wanted to give any concessions to the other. Mom wanted me all to herself, and understandably so, since she was ill. She needed as much support as possible. But my new wife wasn't overly yielding. It was a difficult tug-of-war between my wife and mother but I needed those final years with mama, and I was determined to be the best son I could be. She wasn't perfect, but then who is? Everyone knew her and loved her for who she was.

During my mother's illness, I devoted myself to her as best I could. I took her to her doctor's appointments and did whatever else she needed when she needed it. I even bought her a car just so she could have one with air conditioning. It had been a long time coming but we were finding common-ground and bonding as mother and son. At the risk of sounding selfish, I have to admit there was a part of me that felt cheated because I missed out on all those years with her while she was well and in good health. We were getting closer but there were still barriers and defense mechanisms that kicked in out of habit. I was so used to losing people and failing relationships that I don't think I ever fully disarmed myself and let people in. I always expected to be abandoned sooner or later.

My second marriage failed also, but I continued to take care of and grow closer to my mother. Having that time with her made dealing with my life issues and my two failed marriages easier than it would have been otherwise.

CHAPTER SEVEN

One of the things that most people find remarkable is that I began working in the mental health field in 1989, but I didn't go into treatment and get clean myself until 1995. For six years I played a role in the mental health and rehabilitation of others while I was still dealing with my own issues. I was still using drugs; still undiagnosed with depression; still hadn't undergone any type of treatment for my own illnesses. Looking back I can't help but think that maybe I had to take the long way around. Maybe I had to take the high road to get to this place and this point in time. And now, when I interact with people at mental health facilities I always freely share my story of recovery with them, and let them know that there's hope for them too. I can relate to them because I've been there. I try to give the same support and positive reinforcement that Curtis Gram gave to me when my journey to recovery first began. Sometimes, just an encouraging word and the extension of compassion and understanding goes a long way. As people became more familiar with me, I was developing a reputation as being someone who endeavored to help others without being judgmental. It was very humbling to know that people wanted to hear what I had to say. I like to think that everyone I come in contact with can sense that I genuinely care about their wellbeing. It's such a tremendous blessing to know that I can touch someone's life who may be struggling with some of the same things I've gone through. I've been asked to speak at churches. Parents have asked me to talk to their children. Others have asked me to talk to their brothers, sisters, nieces, nephews, you name it—anyone they thought my story would help. And I never turn anyone down. I've always seized every opportunity I can to share my story of overcoming. I started receiving calls from people all over the country who had heard about me from someone else. To say that it's "humbling" is an understatement. For me to have a message that people want to hear truly amazes me. When I was asked to go to Seattle to speak, I called my dad and said, "Well, dad, one of us finally made it to Seattle."

A local newspaper wanted to do a story about our support team and individual program. They chose to shadow me for a day as I went out into the field to visit with certain clients. At one particular stop, the client told the reporter how much I had helped him with his depression, mental illness and drug issues. As the client innocently went on to say that I helped him so much because I had suffered from similar issues. I got very nervous because at that time, I hadn't told any of my superiors or co-workers about my past drug abuse. Up to that point, I was only sharing my story with clients whom I felt needed to hear it for their own benefit and inspiration. I chose not to tell my superiors or anyone else for fear they would become judgmental and assume things about me before they ever got the chance to know me. So, as the reporter was asking me his list of questions, I felt compelled to just open up and tell him all about my past. After I told him about my own struggles with addiction I couldn't help but wonder if I had made a huge mistake since my boss didn't even know. I was nervous about going back to work that day because now I had to tell my boss. I had no other choice because everything I said was going to be in the newspaper article. So, after I was done calling on clients, I went back to the office and told my boss I needed to speak with her about some information that would be published in the newspaper article about me. I told her everything. She basically asked if I was comfortable airing my dirty laundry (so to speak), and I said I was okay with it because the ultimate goal was (and is) to help and inspire others. If my tarnished past will help someone else, I have no problem putting it out there and letting it be known.

Several months later, a peer specialist position became available. My boss asked if I would be interested in training for it. I jumped at the opportunity and agreed immediately to be signed up for training.

While I was in training I became aware that there was talk among certain staff members about me and my qualifications for the position. Some of them were speculating and saying some pretty insensitive things about **my** mental health and bout with drug addiction. Apparently, there were doubts about my qualifications and capabilities to be a peer specialist. It angered me a bit, but it also hurt my feelings. So, I went to the head of the training department and asked him what I should do about it. He advised me to bring it up at the next class and see what kind of feedback I got from the other peers. I took his advice and I actually got some valuable suggestions and useful information from the other peers that I put to use after training was over. The day I returned to my workplace, there was a meeting. Near the close of the meeting, the boss asked if anyone had anything else to add before we adjourned. I saw this as a chance to have my say and get all the things off my chest that had been gnawing at me since training. I had the floor. This was a defining moment for me to be able to stand up and speak for myself. Remember, I was that withdrawn little boy who wanted to be invisible, and never wanted to be called on in class because I didn't want to be put on display. But that day, I stood up and started out by saying that I knew there had been talk and suppositions about my ability and qualifications to become a peer specialist. I told everyone there that they need not ask around to get information about me, and that whatever anyone wanted to know about me they were free to come to me directly and I would gladly share the story of my life with them.

That was yet another turning point in my life. Life has to be a continual progression if you're going to experience healing. I suffered such inner turmoil just trying to measure up and feel like I was good enough, and as qualified as anyone else. It comes down to having confidence in yourself because sometimes no matter how hard you try you won't measure up to others expectations and what they think you should be. And it's in those times that I've learned it's more important to strive for "self-acceptance" first before you concern yourself with acceptance from others. When I reflect back on my childhood, I remember wishing I was someone else and wanting to just vanish because I couldn't stand looking at myself when I had the bad acne. But the acne was only a contributor to my self-loathing and low self-esteem. There were many other internal things that threw my formative years out of balance, and most of those things carried over into my adult life. In all honesty, there are certain things that can be lifelong struggles we have to deal with, but once you learn coping skills, you can overcome those things and make it through.

When I tell others there's a way to recover, what better example can I give them than myself? I am walking, living, breathing proof that it can be done. Each time I share my story with someone, it inspires them and gives them hope and the encouragement they need to move forward toward their own recovery. I realize that not everyone believes in a Sovereign God; our Maker and Creator, but in my heart I know that I couldn't have survived and made it this far without the help of The Lord. Sometimes I think back to the rough years on the road with my dad and brothers after we left Jersey City. They were some hellish times but I can't help but think that maybe the hardship was the blessing. I refer to it as the "Jonah effect" because it reminds me of how Jonah had to go through a raging storm, three days in the belly of a whale and then be vomited up on the shore in the place he was destined to be in the first place.

Over the years, I've heard of the many tragedies that struck the lives of friends I had before we left Jersey as well as friends I made when I returned. Most of them didn't make it—the streets claimed their lives. Some were shot to death, others were stabbed, some died of AIDS, some are in prison, and some died of drug overdoses. I can't help but think that I would have been numbered among them if God hadn't led my dad to take us away. I'm still here, and not ashamed to say that I believe God used everything that happened to me as a testimony to help someone else. The prevailing worldview does not readily accept the notion of a Majestic Creator who created each of us with a divine purpose in mind, but I do… I believe it. And I believe that we are not only created for a purpose but that it's critical that we be true to it. You don't design your purpose, you discover it.

CHAPTER EIGHT

I must say that sometimes you don't realize how strong your faith is until it's put to the test. That was the case for me when my mother became ill. Even though remembering is sometimes painful, it's one of the beautiful scars. Thinking and speaking of my mother will forever ignite and awaken a sense of loss and grief in me; but I believe these are necessary emotions because they strengthen my faith. I left my job in Atlanta the same day she called and headed to Augusta not knowing what I'd do, how things would be or if I'd even find another job. For that matter, I didn't know what being with my mother would be like. All I knew was I felt like that 5-year-old little boy who left his mother years before and had to get back to her. I had lived with her off and on over the years but it was during my struggles with addiction and depression, so it was as if I stopped developing during those years. I was now sober and in recovery, so I felt like that innocent little boy going back home to Mama. I didn't expect it to be easy—and it wasn't. But after many tears, disagreements, long heart-to-heart discussions and time together, we found a fresh new love for each other. I was able to truly share my heart with her. And before long, I was saying, *"I love you, Ma,"* and she'd say, *"I love you too, Keith"* — she always called me by my middle name. As far back as I can remember, I can't recall a time prior to then that we ever said "I love you" to one another. I used to wonder why my family had to go through so much drama and pain; disappointment and sadness. Why didn't I have a storybook life like so many other kids? But after spending those precious years with my mother I forgot about all the questions I thought I needed answers to because her love — the love we shared and showered on each other was enough to make all my questions disappear. I started to wonder if I'd be able to stay sober and hold on to my sanity if she passed away. I don't mind telling you I was fearful that I wouldn't be able to handle it; I didn't think I was strong enough.

Mama's health was deteriorating and, inevitably, one day her body became too weak to contain her spirit any longer. When the time came for her to leave this earth, she was in the hospital in Florence, SC. I was at her bedside along with other family members, and watched her take her last breath. I remember sobbing like a baby for almost an hour right there in the hospital room. Then I got up and told my family I loved them, and that I had to go. When I got to my car, I rolled all the windows down, put in my Sam

Cooke cd (I always loved Sam Cooke), and cried all the way back to Augusta.

The next morning I surrounded myself with my peers. Many of the coping skills I learned seemed to automatically kick in. I never even thought about using as a means of coping with my mother's death. That's what recovery is all about. You can learn how to cope with things and make decisions without needing the influence of substances. It works if you let it.

Since my mother's passing I've often wondered if I did as much as I could have for her. Did I take care of her as well as I could have? Did I say "I love you" enough? Did I give her all I had to give? These are questions I'll probably always ask myself, but deep down I know that I did the very best I could to show her how important she was to me and how much I loved her. Each day I'm thankful to God for the time He allowed me to spend with her.

I don't take these strolls down Memory Lane very often; I try to keep them to a bare minimum— using them only as a reminder to be thankful for how far I've come and where I am today. I'd be lying if I said I don't occasionally grieve over what could have been, how things were and how things weren't. But I don't wallow in it. Yes, I wish I'd had a better childhood with more stability growing up, but we all have to play the cards we're dealt and move beyond what WAS. When you realize there's hope for you too, it's like a brand new world opens up and all things become new. My parents were in charge of my childhood but I am in charge of my adulthood—it's up to me now. Looking back and allowing the past to hold you back is unproductive and, quite frankly, unfair to you and those you love. Like me, you may have been victimized as a child and allowed what happened to you to affect your own self-esteem. Don't focus on the fact that you may have gotten a less-than-desirable start in life. Maybe you were abandoned or grew up without parents; tossed around from place to place with no real love or stability. I know that some of you reading this book have gone through things that no one should ever have to experience, and though we may never meet face-to-face, we are kindred spirits and my heart goes out to the wounded child inside of you. But just know that God can heal a wounded heart. I realize that not everyone's situation is the same, and what works for some may not work for others. Some of you may still be in a bad living environment and unable to get out and seek help right now because of circumstances beyond your control. But even in those instances you can still work from within—from within yourself. If you're unable to change your external condition, you can still work on your internal condition—and be triumphant.

We have a catchphrase often used in recovery and that is: *"Recovery is a journey not a destination."* I know that (in some way) I'll need to use everything I've learned on my journey for the rest of my life—while thanking God for making me a new man. For those who have not yet put their faith in a higher power, I say – you are what you think you are. If you live your life believing you are the sum total of your diagnosis, nothing anyone says or does will do any good. That's why in an effective recovery environment we focus on strengths not weaknesses. Here's another phrase we use: *"Whatever you focus your energy on you give power to, therefore, focus on what you want to create not what you want to change."*

The dictionary gives several different definitions for the word "Recovery." Below are just a few:

- An act of recovering.
- The regaining of or possibility of regaining something lost or taken away.
- Restoration or return to health from sickness.
- Restoration or return to any former and better state or condition.

The word "Recover" is literally the act of getting something back that you once had. It's a broad term that can sometimes be a little obscure and difficult to understand in certain settings. I, personally, can never go back to what I had or what I was before. For me, recovery means acquiring a new healthy self, and leaving the old self behind. I'm so much better than I ever was before. Our background and circumstances may have influenced who we are, but WE are responsible for who we become.

CHAPTER NINE

I've told my story of recovery to other Peers with similar mental health and/or substance abuse issues. The CPS training has changed my life, as I know it has for many of my fellow Peers. We all share a common goal, and that is to learn how we can better serve others as we continue to take care of ourselves.

Do not find fault with the man who limps
Or stumbles along the road
Unless you have worn the shoes that hurt
Or struggled beneath his load
There may be tacks in his shoes that hurt,
Though hidden away from view
Or the burden he bears, placed on your back,
Might cause you to stumble, too.
Don't sneer at the man who's down today
Unless you have felt the blow
That caused his fall, or felt the same
That only the fallen know

71

You may be strong, but still the blows
That were his, if dealt to you
In the selfsame way at the selfsame time,
Might cause you to stagger, too
Don't be too harsh with the man who sins
Or pelt him with words or stones
Unless you are sure, yea, doubly sure,
That you have no sins of your own
For you know perhaps, if the tempters voice
Should whisper as soft to you
As it did to him when he went astray,
Would cause you to falter, too.

- Author Unknown

There are those in society who look down on people who struggle with addictions and mental health issues. Some go so far as to think that addicts abuse drugs and alcohol because they enjoy it. But those of us who have been there know that isn't true. Today's mental health professionals all seem to agree that addiction, of any kind, is a means of soothing and attempting to quiet some kind of deeply-rooted pain. Drugs and alcohol are typically a method of escape for an individual in the depths of despair who's unable to cope with where life has taken them. There was a time when people with mental illnesses were shunned or locked away. They were viewed as insane and not worthy to walk among the so-called "normal" people. Even in today's modern society, to some degree, there are still those who think that people with mental illnesses and addictions should be banished to institutions and forgotten. Historically, the mentally ill have been viewed with mixed feelings of fear and revulsion. It's heartbreaking to examine some of the historical statistics on how mental illnesses and addictions were viewed down through the ages before it was classified correctly.

It was years before I was diagnosed and realized that I had struggled with a "real" illness. It wasn't something I wanted, asked for, or imagined. Finding out that my problem had a name and that there was help available to me opened a whole new world and gave me a different perspective. Addiction impacted my whole life as well as the lives of those I love and who love me. When you're deep into addiction, you really can't see what's going on outside yourself. It takes such control of you that you honestly can't see what everyone around you sees. It's been said that the addict is the last one to know they're addicted and the last one to take steps to do something about it. It takes a physical, spiritual, mental and emotional toll on you.

What's important to remember is that it is a disease; an illness that should be viewed from a medical perspective as well as a psychological one. There's help… real help. There's hope… real hope. Don't ever be ashamed or embarrassed to seek help. You can make it one step at a time. My journey to healing began when I came to realize I had a treatable disease that had a name.

<u>Taber's Medical Dictionary describes it this way</u>:

ADDICTION: A compulsive and maladaptive dependence on a substance (e.g. alcohol, cocaine, opiates, or tobacco) or a behavior (e.g., gambling). The dependence typically produces adverse psychological, physical, economic, social, or legal ramifications.

MENTAL DISORDER: An imprecise term for a clinically significant behavioral or psychological syndrome or pattern typically associated with either a distressing symptom or impaired function. It is important to remember that different individuals described as having the same mental disorder are not alike in the way they react to their illness and how they need to be treated.

MENTALLY ILL: Affected by any condition that affects mood or behavior, such as depression, dysphoria, personality disorders, phobias, schizophrenia, or substance abuse, among others.

DYSLEXIA: Difficulty using and interpreting written forms of communication by an individual whose vision and general intelligence are otherwise unimpaired. The condition is usually noticed in schoolchildren by the third grade. They can see and recognize letters but have difficulty spelling and writing words. They have no difficulty recognizing the meaning of objects and pictures and typically have no other learning disorders.

Although the exact cause is unknown, evidence suggests that dyslexia may be caused by an inability to break words into sounds and assemble word sounds from written language.

WELLNESS: Good health, as well as its appreciation and enjoyment. Wellness is more than just a lack of disease symptoms; it is a state of mental and physical balance and fitness.

Ability to experience and integrate meaning and purpose in life through connectedness with self, others, art, music, literature, nature, or a power greater than oneself.

చ

We've all heard people say, "I wish I'd known then what I know now." But you can't know things until it's time to know them. Everything has an appointed time and season. First comes the TEST, then the TESTIMONY.

It wasn't always easy for me to share the deepest, darkest moments of my life with others, and it has sometimes been a struggle for me to talk about certain things that I've never talked about publicly before. But, I believe God brought me through the tough times and raised me up so that I could reach back and help someone else.

The following statements were created by the Appalachian Consultant Group with approval by Mr. Ike Powell:

1. What a person believes about Himself or Herself because He or She has a diagnosis of mental illness can often be more disabling than the illness itself!

3. When one lives without Hope, the willingness to <u>do</u> is paralyzed. It is being disabled not by illness or disease, but by despair!

4. When people are having difficulty seeing Recovery as part of their lives, they need to be surrounded with the possibility of Recovery!

5. Everyone has the ability to grow and change, therefore, if I relate to a person's Potential, there's the possibility of calling forth GREATNESS!

6. When I see how much you have overcome to get to where you are today, I Know you are a WALKING MIRACLE!

7. The greatest barriers to Recovery are often the negative messages that reinforce a person's negative self-image and negative self-talk!

Dr. Mary Ellen Copeland's five (5) key recovery concepts are:

1) Hope
2) Personal Responsibility
3) Education
4) Self Advocacy
5) Support

These concepts are vital, key elements of recovery. **Hope;** where there's life there's always Hope. One of the many feelings an addict experiences is a sense of hopelessness. I know the feeling well. Feeling there was no hope for me was one of the reasons for my two suicide attempts. But, I'm here today thriving and recovering and sharing with as many people as I can the fact that they too can overcome and be whole. When it comes to **Personal Responsibility,** it's important that "you" as an individual not expect others to assume the responsibility for "your" recovery. You must take the first step. **Education** is also very important because you need to learn coping skills and other things to help you get through tough times. **Self-advocacy,** in a broad sense, is the act of caring and speaking up for yourself; it has nothing to do with selfishness. It's about making the best decisions and choices that enable and empower you to be the best you can be. Finally, **Support.** You can't go it alone. I wouldn't have made it without the love and support of my family, professional/personal intervention, treatment, etc. You need a strong support system.

I believe God places people in our paths and in our lives for a specific purpose and at a specific time. I owe a personal debt of gratitude, first and foremost, to God Almighty, and to Mr. Curtis Gram, who stuck with me and was always there for me through all my struggles. The wisdom, guidance and encouragement he gave me can never fully be put into words. I've known him for more than fifteen years now and still keep in contact with him because he is a constant reminder of how blessings flow. Each day I strive to live my life in such a way that I will be a blessing to others as Curtis was to me. He was a major driving force in my life at a time when it felt like I was the only one on earth who knew that kind of dark despair. Curtis knew how I felt because he had *been there*—he knew exactly where I was.

After going through training and becoming a Certified Peer Specialist, I finally understand what Curtis was trying to convey years ago when he told this mentally ill, drug addicted young man to look in the mirror and say:

"I am somebody, I love myself, there is no one better than me."

Not only did I begin to say and believe it, I started living it. And I became an active participant in the recovery of others as well as in my own. I got involved in positive activities and aligned myself with positive, re-enforcing people. That's an important component of recovery.

One of the many inspirational activities I became a part of was music therapy. There's a saying from a poem that was written sometime around the 16th century, which states, in part, that *'music has charms to soothe the savage beast.'* It may be slightly misquoted but soothing music truly does calm and soothe the soul. In the book of I Samuel, Saul was tormented by an evil spirit, and told his servants to find someone skilled in playing music. They brought David who played the harp so beautifully that the evil spirit would depart from Saul whenever David played for him.

Being part of a music therapy group gave me the opportunity to do something I love. Music and singing have always been a big part of my life. The music therapy group that I'm proud to be a part of is made up of veterans and clinicians who make music for the "health of it." We play for hospital events and various other events throughout the community. Music has a way of touching the deepest, innermost part of your being.

THORNS CANNOT DIMINISH THE BEAUTY OF A
ROSE.

CHAPTER TEN

You may be in a place in life where you think there's no hope for you; you've just about given up on ever being whole and feeling good about life and yourself. I know that feeling, I was there. You may be struggling with drug addiction, alcoholism, mental health issues or both, and you think that's how your life will always be. But I'm living proof that it doesn't have to be that way; it isn't carved in stone. There's hope for you too. You have to meet the challenges; face the giants head-on and give it all you've got. It's never too late or too early to begin your journey to recovery. You can start from wherever you are.

Sometimes you have to work from the inside out. If you're harboring resentment or animosity of any kind, let it go. Learn to forgive. Forgive those who have wronged you, whether it be family, friends, acquaintances, whomever—forgive them. But most of all, forgive yourself. Realize that "you" are somebody and there's no one better than you.

I've been in the deepest darkest pit, been incarcerated, and had three failed marriages. BUT, failing "at" something doesn't mean <u>you</u> are a failure. It doesn't define who you are or what you can accomplish. Think of failure as a way of eliminating things that didn't work.

The Creator of heaven and earth gave us the freedom to ultimately choose the road we want to travel in this life. We can choose the road to wholeness and healing or the one to darkness and despair. We either run toward God or away from HIM—there's no other direction.

MY LIFE HAS BEAUTIFUL SCARS

I've devoted the last half of this book to *quotes and reflections*.

It's no surprise that many quotes are referred to as **Inspirational**. Throughout history there have been those who have inspired us more than they'll ever know—and with only a few words.

Some of the greatest words of wisdom were written during the writer's darkest hours. It's in the deep recesses of a troubled soul that reflective thoughts are conceived and birthed. If you read the Psalms or listen to hymns that have been written and sung down through the years, it's evident that wisdom and strength grow during times of great trial, grief and sorrow—when your heart is heavy. It's comforting to know that others have weathered the storms of life and made it safely to shore.

Encouragement is one of the greatest gifts you can give to someone. Not everyone will receive (or perceive) the same message from these quotes, but each statement is a testimonial with its own depth and fruitfulness.

The authors of these thought-provoking statements are mostly unknown. It's possible that their goal was simply to inspire and encourage others without wanting any credit or anything in return. That's a code we should all live by, and how I've chosen to live my life. It's why I share my story and try never to miss an opportunity to lift someone up.

I don't know the authorship for each of the quotes that follow, but I hope they'll inspire you as they have inspired me.

I've added a journal-type portion that I hope you'll use as a place to chronicle and express your own personal thoughts and feelings.

The majority of participants in support groups are encouraged to keep journals and refer back to them often to chart emotional progress. A journal is like a window to your soul; a way of giving your innermost feelings an outlet and a place where your deepest thoughts can be expressed without fear of judgment, shame or the need for explanation. That's why I've called this section, **REFLECTIONS**. When we reflect on something it causes us to pause and think about things that may need to be dealt with.

Footnote: Quotes used in the [**Reflections**] section of this book have circulated (both online and offline) over the years, and are full of wisdom and insight. However, it's difficult to pinpoint the exact origin of them. I do not, by any means, claim ownership or authorship of them. Therefore, credit and recognition are given to each individual author though their identity is unknown to me.

REFLECTIONS

"Live as if you were to die tomorrow; learn as if you were to live forever."

Your thoughts, hopes, dreams and personal reflections:

_____

_____

_____

_____

_____

_____

_____

_____

_____

BEAUTIFUL SCARS

REFLECTIONS

"We must be the change we wish to see in the world."

Your thoughts, hopes, dreams and personal reflections:

_____

_____

_____

_____

_____

_____

_____

_____

_____

_____

Brian Keith Anderson

BEAULTIFUL SCARS

REFLECTIONS

"It takes a village to raise a child, but sick villages raise sick children."

Your thoughts, hopes, dreams and personal reflections:

_____

_____

_____

_____

_____

_____

_____

_____

_____

_____

Brian Keith Anderson

REFLECTIONS

"Don't let your past be just ordinary. Don't lose the excitement of what God has done for you."

Your thoughts, hopes, dreams and personal reflections:

_____

_____

_____

_____

_____

_____

_____

_____

_____

_____

BEAUTIFUL SCARS

Brian Keith Anderson

REFLECTIONS

"Slow down; God is still in heaven. You don't have to do everything by yourself. Let go and let God."

Your thoughts, hopes, dreams and personal reflections:

_____

_____

_____

_____

_____

_____

_____

_____

_____

_____

BEACUTIFUL SCARS

(blank lined page)

REFLECTIONS

"When GOD solves your problems, you have faith in HIS abilities; but if GOD doesn't solve your problems maybe HE has faith in your abilities."

Your thoughts, hopes, dreams and personal reflections:

_____

_____

_____

_____

_____

_____

_____

_____

_____

_____

_____

Brian Keith Anderson

BEAUTIFUL SCARS

REFLECTIONS

"Remember a happy, peaceful time in your life and rest there. Each moment has richness that takes a lifetime to savor."

Your thoughts, hopes, dreams and personal reflections:

_____

_____

_____

_____

_____

_____

_____

_____

_____

_____

_____

_____

BEAUTIFUL SCARS

REFLECTIONS

"Watch water flow, watch corn grow, watch the leaves blow... take nothing for granted."

Your thoughts, hopes, dreams and personal reflections:

_____

_____

_____

_____

_____

_____

_____

_____

_____

_____

_____

BEAUTIFUL SCARS

Brian Keith Anderson

REFLECTIONS

"Notice the sun and the moon as they rise and set. They are remarkable for their steady pattern of movement, not their speed."

Your thoughts, hopes, dreams and personal reflections:

_____

_____

_____

_____

_____

_____

_____

_____

_____

_____

_____

BEAUTIFUL SCARS

REFLECTIONS

"Quit planning how you're going to use what you know, learn, or possess. God's gifts just are; be grateful and their purpose will become clear."

Your thoughts, hopes, dreams and personal reflections:

_____

_____

_____

_____

_____

_____

_____

_____

_____

_____

BEAUTIFUL SCARS

REFLECTIONS

"Don't labor over things you want to say; words will spring up naturally if you let them."

Your thoughts, hopes, dreams and personal reflections:

_____

_____

_____

_____

_____

_____

_____

_____

_____

_____

_____

BEAUTIFUL SCARS

_____

_____

_____

_____

_____

_____

_____

_____

_____

_____

_____

_____

_____

_____

_____

_____

_____

_____

_____

_____

_____

_____

_____

_____

REFLECTIONS

"Allow yourself to have quiet time. Rest isn't a luxury, it's a necessity."

Your thoughts, hopes, dreams and personal reflections:

_____

_____

_____

_____

_____

_____

_____

_____

_____

_____

_____

119

BEAUTIFUL SCARS

REFLECTIONS

"Communication isn't measured by words alone."

Your thoughts, hopes, dreams and personal reflections:

_____

_____

_____

_____

_____

_____

_____

_____

_____

_____

_____

BEAUTIFUL SCARS

REFLECTIONS

"Be spontaneous sometimes. Life is for living, not always scheduling."

Your thoughts, hopes, dreams and personal reflections:

_____

_____

_____

_____

_____

_____

_____

_____

_____

_____

_____

BEAUTIFUL SCARS

REFLECTIONS

"Listen to the song of a bird; the complete song. Music and nature are gifts, but only if you are willing to receive them."

Your thoughts, hopes, dreams and personal reflections:

_____

_____

_____

_____

_____

_____

_____

_____

_____

_____

_____

_____

BEAUTIFUL SCARS

REFLECTIONS

"Take time just to think, reflect, ponder, and mull."

Your thoughts, hopes, dreams and personal reflections:

_____

_____

_____

_____

_____

_____

_____

_____

_____

_____

_____

Brian Keith Anderson

BEAUTIFUL SCARS

REFLECTIONS

"Make time for play at the things you like to do. Whatever your age, your inner child needs recreation."

Your thoughts, hopes, dreams and personal reflections:

_____

_____

_____

_____

_____

_____

_____

_____

_____

_____

_____

BEAUTIFUL SCARS

REFLECTIONS

"Listen to the words you speak, especially in prayer."

Your thoughts, hopes, dreams and personal reflections:

_____

_____

_____

_____

_____

_____

_____

_____

_____

_____

BEAUTIFUL SCARS

REFLECTIONS

"Pace yourself. God took six days to create the universe and rested on the seventh. The Creator rested and so should we."

Your thoughts, hopes, dreams and personal reflections:

_____

_____

_____

_____

_____

_____

_____

_____

_____

_____

_____

BEAUTIFUL SCARS

Brian Keith Anderson

REFLECTIONS

"Take time to read the Bible; it enriches and provokes thought."

Your thoughts, hopes, dreams and personal reflections:

_____

_____

_____

_____

_____

_____

_____

_____

_____

_____

BEAUTIFUL SCARS

REFLECTIONS

"Direct your life with purposeful choices."

Your thoughts, hopes, dreams and personal reflections:

_____

_____

_____

_____

_____

_____

_____

_____

_____

_____

_____

BEAUTIFUL SCARS

REFLECTIONS

"Take time to wonder. Without wonder, life is merely existence."

Your thoughts, hopes, dreams and personal reflections:

_____

_____

_____

_____

_____

_____

_____

_____

_____

_____

_____

Brian Keith Anderson

_____

_____

_____

_____

_____

_____

_____

_____

_____

_____

_____

_____

_____

_____

_____

_____

_____

_____

_____

_____

_____

BEAUTIFUL SCARS

REFLECTIONS

"Let go of the past. It's gone."

Your thoughts, hopes, dreams and personal reflections:

_____

_____

_____

_____

_____

_____

_____

_____

_____

_____

_____

Brian Keith Anderson

REFLECTIONS

"Count your friends. If you have one, you are blessed. If you have more, you are truly blessed. Bless them in return."

Your thoughts, hopes, dreams and personal reflections:

_____

_____

_____

_____

_____

_____

_____

_____

_____

_____

_____

Brian Keith Anderson

REFLECTIONS

"Count your blessings - one at a time and slowly."

Your thoughts, hopes, dreams and personal reflections:

_____

_____

_____

_____

_____

_____

_____

_____

_____

_____

_____

_____

BEAUTIFUL SCARS

REFLECTIONS

"Prayer is not a "spare wheel" that you pull out when in trouble, but it is a "steering wheel" that directs the right path throughout the journey."

Your thoughts, hopes, dreams and personal reflections:

_____

_____

_____

_____

_____

_____

_____

_____

_____

_____

_____

BEAUTIFUL SCARS

Brian Keith Anderson

REFLECTIONS

"Why is a car's Windshield so large and the Rearview mirror so small? Because our PAST is not as important as our FUTURE. So, look ahead and move on."

Your thoughts, hopes, dreams and personal reflections:

_____

_____

_____

_____

_____

_____

_____

_____

_____

_____

_____

BEAUTIFUL SCARS

REFLECTIONS

"Friendship is like a BOOK. It can take years to write but only a few minutes to burn."

Your thoughts, hopes, dreams and personal reflections:

_____

_____

_____

_____

_____

_____

_____

_____

_____

_____

Brian Keith Anderson

BEANUTIFUL SCARS

Brian Keith Anderson

REFLECTIONS

"WORRYING does not take away tomorrow's TROUBLES, it takes away today's PEACE."

Your thoughts, hopes, dreams and personal reflections:

_____

_____

_____

_____

_____

_____

_____

_____

_____

_____

_____

_____

BEAUTIFUL SCARS

Brian Keith Anderson